D0976995

Are You My Uber?

A Parody

by Sarah Dooley
illustrated by hilary fitzgerald campbell

RUNNING PRESS

PHILADELPHIA

For Mom, Dad, and Julia, who give me all my best ideas.
And I guess also for Molly and Elliot (those were our dogs)
(they're dead now) (oof, sorry!!).—**S.D.**

For Lily —**H.F.C.**

Running Press
Hachette Book Group
1290 Avenue of the Americas, New York, NY 10104
www.runningpress.com
@Running_Press

Printed in China

First Edition: October 2019

Published by Running Press, an imprint of Perseus Books, LLC,
a subsidiary of Hachette Book Group, Inc. The Running Press name
and logo are trademarks of the Hachette Book Group.

The Hachette Speakers Bureau provides a wide range of authors for speaking events. To find
out more, go to www.hachettespeakersbureau.com or call (866) 376-6591

The publisher is not responsible for websites (or their content)
that are not owned by the publisher.

Print book cover and interior design by name Frances J. Soo Ping Chow.

ISBNs: 978-0-7624-9646-4 (hardcover), 978-0-7624-9647-1 (ebook),
978-0-7624-9853-6 (ebook), 978-0-7624-9854-3 (ebook)

RRD-S

11   10   9   8   7   6   5   4   3   2

This book is a parody and has not been prepared, approved, or authorized by the
author of *Are You My Mother?* or his heirs or representatives.

AUTHOR'S NOTE

One time I thought I was getting into my Uber but it turned out to be a family's SUV full of children. They were not very happy and I was very embarrassed. (Don't be like me: to avoid an Uber mix-up and stay safe, make sure you're getting into the right car with the right driver by matching the license plate, car make and model, and driver photo with the info in your app, and always ask the driver to confirm your name before you get into the car.)

In that moment I felt a lot like the lost, confused baby bird in P.D. Eastman's *Are You My Mother?*, one of my childhood favorites. In the same way the newborn bird in the original book asks a number of farm animals and objects that clearly are not his mother if they are, the man in *Are You My Uber?* encounters a succession of iconic NYC vehicles and characters, increasing in their absurdity, who consistently inform him that they are, in fact, not his Uber. In this way, the book is an expression of how we can all feel lost in the world sometimes, like little baby birds. But it's okay! It could be worse. Baby birds are *sooo* cute. Pass the worms.

A man got off a midnight bus at Port Authority.
He had never been to New York before. He needed to get uptown.

He looked at his phone.
"Where is my Uber?" he said.

He looked up. He did not see it.
He looked down. He did not see it.

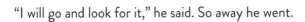

"I will go and look for it," he said. So away he went.

He did not know what his Uber looked like.
It said it was a Ford Taurus.
He did not know what a Ford Taurus looked like.

He went right by it.
He did not see it.

He came to an off-duty cab.
"Are you my Uber?" he said to the off-duty cab.

The driver just looked and looked. He did not say a thing.
The off-duty cab was not his Uber, so he went on.

Then he came to a hearse.
"Are you my Uber?"

"Are you dead?" asked the driver. The man shook his head.
"Then no."

The off-duty cab was not his Uber.

The hearse was not his Uber.

So the man went on.
"I have to find my Uber!" he said. "But where? Where is it?
Where could it be?"

Then he came to a halal cart. "Are you my Uber?"
"I am not your Uber. This is a halal cart. Do you want hot sauce?"

The off-duty cab was not his Uber, the hearse was not his Uber,
and the halal cart was not his Uber.
So the man went on.

Now he came to a horse cop.

"Are you my Uber?"

"Neigh."

Did he *have* an Uber?
"I did have an Uber. I know I did. I will find it. I WILL."
Now the man did not walk. He ran!

Then he saw a woman painted to look like the Statue of Liberty.
She was pushing a shopping cart full of cats dressed up as presidents.

Could that thing be his Uber?
"Are you my Uber?"

"I AM AN ARTIST!!!!!!!!!!!!!!!!"

No, she was not. The man was scared. He ran on and on.

Now he looked way, way down the block.
He saw a mattress being carried by a bunch of rats.

"There it is!" said the man.
He called to the rats but the rats did not stop. The rats went on.

He looked way, way up. He saw a drone.
"Here I am, Uber!" he called out.
But the drone did not stop. The drone went on. So he kept going.

Just then, the man saw a big thing.
This must be his Uber!
"There it is!" he said. "There is my Uber!"

He ran right up to it. "Uber, Uber!
Here I am, Uber!" he said to the big thing.
But the big thing just said, "Chop chop chop."
"Oh, you are not my Uber," said the man.
"You are a Chop. I have to get out of here!"

But the man could not get away.
His shirt was caught in the door!
The Chop went up.

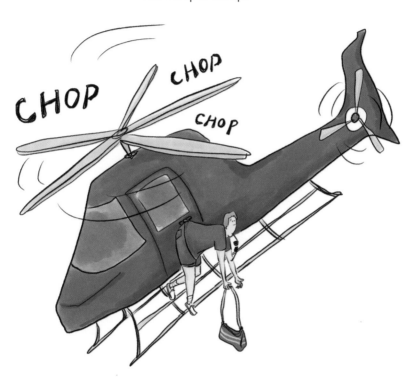

It went way, way up. And up, up, up went the man.

Just then, someone pulled him inside.
"Are you my Uber?" the man asked.
"No. I'm Billy Joel."
But now, where was the Billy Joel going?

"I want my Uber! I want to go uptown!"
Just then, they came to a stop mid-air.
"Let me guess, you're going uptown to meet a girl? Real original,"
he said. "I've heard *that* one before."

Then, something happened.
The Billy Joel dropped the man off on the curb
just as his Uber pulled up.

"Do you know who I am?" the driver asked.
"Yes, I know who you are.

You are not an off-duty cab, you are not a hearse.

You are not a halal cart, you are not a horse cop.
You are not a Billy Joel.

Your name is Doug, you drive a Ford Taurus, and you are my Uber."

The driver stared at him.
The Uber smelled very strongly of cologne,
but it took him straight uptown.

The man was happy.

The End.